I0163661

the RETURN OF the DAYS OF NOAh AND the DAYS OF SODOM AND GOMORRAh COME TOGETHER

The Return of the Days of Noah

ISBN:978-0-9904360-8-9
Soft cover

Copyright © 2016 by Joshua International
dba H.A.Lewis Ministries

This book was printed in the United
States of America.

THE RETURN
OF THE
DAYS OF NOAH

**"Woe to you who long for
the day of the Lord!"
-Amos 5:18**

H.A. LEWIS

INTRODUCTION

This book has been written in hopes it will open the heart, mind, and spirit of everyone who reads this book it so they will clearly understand the times we are dealing in and what we are facing.

I Kings 8:61

And may your hearts be fully committed to the LORD our God, to live by his decrees and obey his commands, as at this time."

CONTENTS

A battle between two Kingdoms

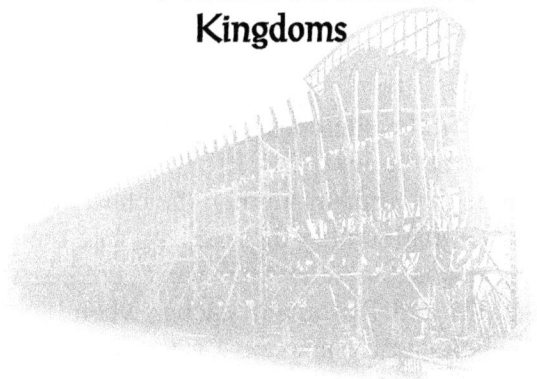

Chapter 1
The War is On
>>>>>>>>>>>>>>>>>>>>>

This earth is beginning to revert back to the days of Noah and the days of Sodom and Gomorrah.

In the churches today there is a lot of talk about the Jezebel spirit, the Ahab spirit, and the different strongmen the churches are facing. In all reality these spirits, like the Jezebel spirit and the Ahab spirit, are not what the Old Testament teaches when talking about the ancient spirits. These are human beings that were affected by these particular spirits.

There is a movement in the spiritual world today, or rather unrest so to say, because the enemy knows his time is short.

Satan is bringing his strongest
lieutenants back.

He does not have much time to accomplish what he wants to accomplish so he's bringing his strongest lieutenants back.

The Bible says it would be as the days of Noah in the days the Son of man returns. In other words in the time that Jesus chooses to return back for His church conditions on the earth will be like they were in the days of Noah and in the days of Sodom and Gomorrah. There will be chaos and confusion, perversion, disorder, and rebellion everywhere.

These same spirits, which were responsible for how things were in the time of Noah, Lot, and Sodom and Gomorrah, will be manipulating behind the scenes in today's time and era.

Studying the Old Testament we hear different names of false gods that were worshipped by different nations. For example, there was the god, Moloch, who was worshipped by the Philistines. There

9

were other false gods like *Dagon* and *Baal*. Baal was the rival to Jehovah in the Old Testament. Israel got carried away into Baal worship and God sent them into punishment because of it.

The Philistines would offer their children to *Moloch*. They had a big statue made of brass that they would heat until the hands of the statue got red hot. As the statue's hands glowed from the heat of the fires that were burning within, the parents would take their infant up and place them in the hands of the statue as an offering to Moloch.

There were also spirits like the prince of Mede and Persia, which you find in the Old Testament in the book of Daniel. Daniel begins to pray and fast on the behalf of the nation of Israel to find out what is going to be happening. Twenty-one days into his praying and fasting the angel Gabriel appears to him and says, "Daniel, beloved of the Lord, on the very first day the Lord heard your prayers and I was sent to bring you the answer but as I came, I was held up by the prince of Persia."

What is the prince of Persia? The prince of Persia is a fallen angel that is ruling and reigning with Lucifer in the second heaven. These fallen angels that are part of the army of Satan have a different assignment each. They are lords over the different areas of the earth.

Now the prince of Mede and Persia was responsible for the military of Persia and responsible for the victories that the Persians were having over their different enemies. When Gabriel was finally able to get through because Michael the archangel was sent to help him, he was able to come down and give the message to Daniel and then said to Daniel, "I need now to return to continue the battle with this prince that was over the area."

Today we makeup different strongmen, like the strongman of alcoholism, the strongman of the occult, the Jezebel spirit, the Ahab spirit, this spirit, and that spirit. I understand the church has problems with these different kinds of spirits but realize this, that the Jezebel spirit is a spirit of rebellion. It is not the original strongman; it is subjected to the original strongman. It follows its commander's order. We can deal with the Jezebel spirit by praying against it, binding it, and casting it out; however, until we deal with the power behind that spirit we'll not have total victory.

We need to be aware of the names of these strongmen because then we will have the power to bind them and gain victory over them so the people will be set free.

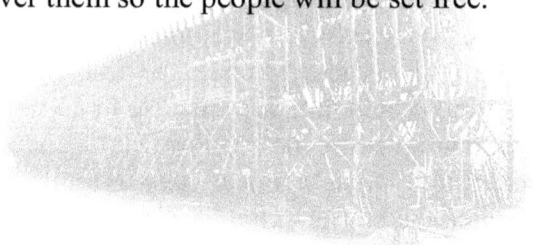

Instead of fighting foot soldiers, were going to
be fighting THE GENERALS.

Where did these strongmen originally come
from and what is their purpose now?

Chapter 2
The Origin of the Strongmen
>>>>>>>>>>>>>>>>>>>>>>>>
What is their purpose?

In Genesis 6 we read about the sons of God who are observing the daughters of men. They find these women very appealing to them and make a decision to leave their first estate to intermingle with human women. They have relationships with these women and giants are born. These angels that left their first estate are the strongmen over different areas of this globe.

In the record of Enoch, which was rejected from being canonized because they did not feel that it passed the test of a canonized book. In other words, it was not one hundred percent accurate in geography, history, cultural, spiritual, or science. There was something that was not quite completed so they debated for a long time. The book of Enoch was almost canonized and for a while it was and then it was rejected and taken out. It was considered to be an Old Testament apocrypha, just a book of history or cultural legends.

However, in the book of Enoch, he writes about the watchers. He records that there were two hundred watchers in total and these watchers were angels that were sent to observe things that were happening on the earth. As they were watching and observing, they began to notice the daughters of men. The leader, whose name was Semyaza, according to Hebrew tradition, decided that he was going to take an earthly woman and have relationship with her. He told his ideas to the others that were overlords of the two hundred.

He said, "I fear I will make this decision on my own then I will have to stand in judgment by myself." The other leaders made a promise, twenty in all, that they would follow his example and they would also select a woman to have a relationship with and eventually all 200 of these watchers followed the example of their leader, Semyaza, and they began to have relationships.

According to the book of Enoch the children produced by these watchers and the earthly women were three hundred cubits in height. They ate all the food that man could provide for them, but they weren't getting enough so they turned on the human race and began to eat birds and animals. Basically they ate whatever they could get their hands on and eventually they began to eat human beings, which is where cannibalism came in.

Finally God had enough with the pollution of these creatures and the rebellion of man. He talked to Noah, the only righteous man of his generation, and told him to build the ark. Noah did and he and his family entered into the ark, where God closed the door. Then God destroyed all life on the surface of the earth, doing away with these offspring of the fallen angels and the daughters of men.

Now this should have ended the problem right then, but after the flood when mankind started to repopulate the earth the same problem arose. The angels, which were not destroyed in the flood, once again made the decision they were going to have relationship with human women. And giants were produced again.

Each and every one of these giants born to these fallen angels and women is the origin of your false gods and goddesses. Can you imagine what it was like to be an average man during that time and see a giant? During that time the average height of man was about four feet eleven inches. If you were lucky you would have been about five feet. Your weight would have been somewhere around one hundred ten to one hundred twenty pounds. Men were not big in size whatsoever.

Let's say you're going on a journey and suddenly you see a creature that looks like a human being but it's standing over thirteen feet in height and weighing in the hundreds of pounds. Immediately you consider that this thing is a god because of its great size and strength. You've never seen anything like this in your entire life.

No one in the village you grew up in looked like this. You begin to worship this creature because of its size, strength, and power.

These giants became legends.

Nimrod became Hercules or Heracles, the demigod of strength, power, and might to the Greeks and the Romans

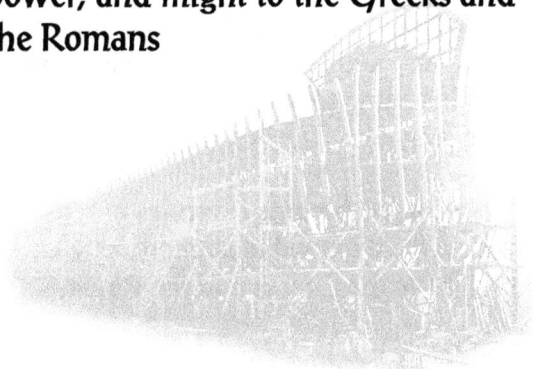

CHAPTER 3
The Legendary Giant
>>>>>>>>>>>>>>>>>>>>>>>

For instance, *Nimrod* was a giant and he was worshipped because of his strength and his knowledge of warfare. As Nimrod with his army conquered different areas, the legend of Nimrod began to spread among the different cultures. Of course they would change his name to a name that was suitable to their language.

Nimrod became Hercules or Heracles, the demigod of strength, power, and might to the Greeks and the Romans.

He was quite famous because of the skin of the lion he wore across his shoulders. The skin was from a lion he had killed his bare hands.

Wherever this young man with the lion skin across his shoulders went, he was immediately recognized as the great Hercules.

His name meant the *bespeckled* one because of the spots on the coat of the lion he wore. Some translations believe it was the skin of a leopard. Either way, if you kill a leopard or a lion with your hands and a spear, you have accomplished something.

That mantle he had across his shoulders was a sign of who he was.

Everybody knew him because of that skin. *Heracles or Hercules* means the **bespeckled one**. *Orisis*, the Egyptian god also means the *bespeckled* one.

Therefore, *Osiris and Isis*, the Egyptian god and goddess, are actually *Nimrod* and his wife, *Semiramis*.

See how his fame grows in different cultures? They just changed his name. Just as his name changed so did his wife, Semiramis.

Not only was she his wife but she was also his mother.

21

And in every culture in the world you have a statue of a *Madonna* a young woman holding her infant in her hands. In Catholic tradition it is *Mary*, the mother of Jesus.

In China, it is their virtuous saint holding their god in her arms.

In India it is *Kali* holding *Ganesh* in her arms.

No matter the culture or the name, it's the same being.

People, like *Semiramis and Nimrod*, are the ones responsible for developing these demigods or these false gods.

There was an angel called, **Azazyel** that taught men how to make weapons of war like swords, knives, shields, and breastplates.

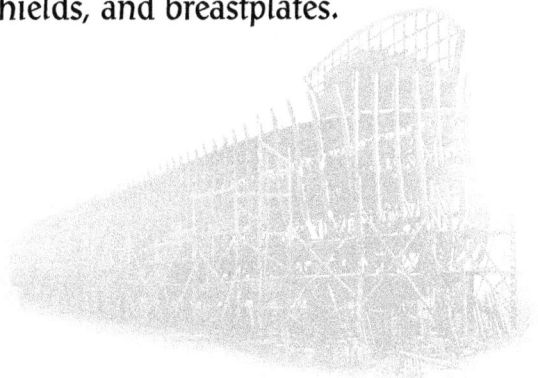

Chapter 4
The sons of God Intermarrying
>>>>>>>>>>>>>>>>>>>>>>>

These angels that were intermarrying with the women on the face of the earth became the power over the atmosphere and over different countries, villages, and cities. Each and every one of these angels taught something to the women they were having the relationship with.

There was an angel called, *Azazyel* that taught men how to make weapons of war like swords, knives, shields, and breastplates.

For the women, he taught how make mirrors, how to do eye shadow and all kinds of dye. They could dye their clothes a different color and they even dyed their hair. *Azazyel* brought all this into existence on the earth. This is what he taught the women that he was having relationships with.

Another angel named *Amazarak* taught sorcery and the dividing of roots and herbology to the woman he had a relationship with. He taught man how to mix different roots together to produce different spells. He also introduced the occult science in the world.

Armers is another angel who taught the solution of sorcery. In other words, he taught the different formulas they would use in casting spells and in making drugs. He taught them how to put these combinations together to produce the chemicals needed to bring the spell to fulfillment.

The names of these watchers are all Hebrew names found in Hebrew tradition, history, and legend.

To better understand this we would have to research many different books like the apocrypha, the uncanonized books.

These interesting tales that are told are rooted in truth, but they have become legends or fables over the years.

This one particular angel, Barkayal, taught the observing of the stars.

He showed men the constellations taught them about the twelve houses of the zodiac. Then there was *Akibeel* who taught the signs and wonders of the heavens and what they meant. *Tamiel* taught astronomy, the study of the heavenly bodies, the stars, the cosmos, the milky ways and all the science they did not know before this spirit entered into the earth.

The spirit, Asaradel, taught the motion of the moon.

He taught man that the moon affected the personalities and moods of human beings. He taught them about the crescent moon, the waning moon, the waxing moon, the full moon, and the new moon. He taught them the occult science of following the moon. These watchers began to exert their authority and the people began to worship them as gods. They were the power behind all the earthbound spirits. They controlled these demon spirits by telling them what to do, how to do it, and how to enter human beings and take over.

The so-called two hundred watchers, according to the book of Enoch, were directly under Lucifer.

They had different areas of the world to be in charge of and of course they had many demons, earthbound spirits that were under their authority. They operated according to the instructions given to them. Above these spirits, these earthbound spirits there would be a leader and that leader was a strongman.

There were ranks just like in the military. The order of the Unseen World

At the bottom were the **privates**, then the **corporals**; next were **sergeants**, then **master sergeants**, and **tech sergeants**.

Afterwards there were positions like lieutenants, captains, majors, colonels, and then generals. There is a line of order and everything is organized and functions according to the plan of the general that is in charge of a particular section

It's the same way in the spirit world

There are minor demons running around carrying out the plans of the spirit that is directly above them and all the way up to the strongman.

Sergeants

Now the Jezebel spirits, Ahab spirits and these other spirits, are called strongmen whom we are facing today. They are like the **sergeants** in the military. They are strongmen to a point; however, they are **Not the ruling spirits.** We need to know the spirits behind them so that we can come against them, we can bind them.

It's interesting to study the names of the watchers named in the book of Enoch.

Each of these 20 spirits were in charge of 10 spirits and gave them their orders by telling them what to do, where to go, and what not to do.

Here's a look at some of the names

Samyaza is the lead spirit and the absolute strongman over the strongmen;

1. Urakabarameel
2. Akibeel
3. Tamiel
4. Ramuel
5. Danel
6. Azkeel
7. Saraknyal
8. Asael
9. Armers
10. Batraal
11. Anane
12. Zavebe
13. Samsaveel
14. Ertael
15. Turel
16. Yomyael
17. Arazyal.

Studying the book of Enoch definitely
gives a lot of insight into the spiritual word
and each of these watchers introduced
something to the world that helped to lead
man further in his rebellion

THE RETURN OF THE DAYS OF NOAH

Chapter 5
Identifying the Opponent
For Heavens Sake

>>>>>>>>>>>>>>>>>>>>>>>

A couple of years back my wife and I were ministering in Switzerland and we met this wonderful couple. The husband was a teacher and his wife was a police officer. They were all excited because she had just found out she was pregnant. They had been praying for a few years for her to become pregnant so they would have a child. Of course we were excited for them and we prayed for them. My wife and I strongly felt that God was going to bless her with a child.

We continued to minister and then returned back to the States. We were not back in the States for very long when we got a phone call from the couple. They were distraught because she was losing the baby. My wife and I promised to pray and we began to intercede for them but she lost the baby due to a miscarriage. We wondered, "Lord, what happened? We were sincere.

We were asking You to spare them this grief and to have mercy."

The Lord said to us, "You did not bind the strongman. You did not call the spirit by name."

I said, "What do you mean Lord?"

He said, "When you prayed you were doing shotgun prayers." It was like I was shooting at anything in the dark hoping I'd hit something.

He said, "I don't want shotgun prayers. I want you to be focused so that when you pray you hit the mark every time. There is a strongman that is over this and you know the name of the spirit because you have studied the book of Enoch and you studied about the watchers and the angels that left their first estate. Now go back and restudy your research."

I went back to the book of Enoch and there was the name of an angel called *Kasdaye*l. It said that this particular spirit taught woman how to terminate the life within the womb.

This was the strong man over the spirit of abortion or miscarriage. He was the strongman behind the deity known as Moloch, the god of sacrifice.

Well the woman from Switzerland became pregnant again, and we went into sincere prayer because she was having trouble again. We bound that spirit by name and called out the name to the Lord. We got the attention of the strongman and we said, "Lord, we take authority over *Kasdayel* and we bind it in Jesus name. He has no power to cause this life to be terminated." She gave birth to a beautiful baby son.

The Lord said, "When you know the name of the strongman, it's like shooting a .22 at that person. You hit it every time."

When we just say general prayers we are not really going to hit anything. When we pray we need to be disciplined. Many preachers will say we are making a big thing out of this but if you're going to deal with the strongman deal with the real strongman.

34

The Lord never shows us something to waste our time. He shows it so we will learn a lesson and apply it.

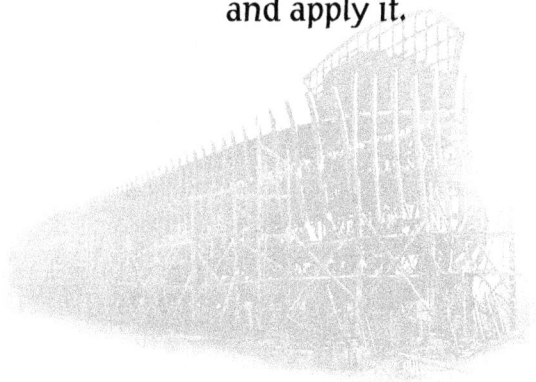

Chapter 6
In the Book of Daniel
>>>>>>>>>>>>>>>>>>>>>>>>

God began to show me in the Old Testament the powers that were over different countries. The Lord never shows us something to waste our time. He shows it so we will learn a lesson. I began to see a prince over the nation of Babylon. This prince had power over the king and over the leaders of the nation of Babylon. He would push out lesser spirits to expand his kingdom. As long as he was in power, nobody could take the authority away from the earthly king ruling that particular nation and other nations that were conquered because of this strongman giving his power to the military of this earthly king.

The king of Babylon, Nebuchadnezzar, conquered the whole known civilization of his time. He had a strongman that he worshipped, and he commanded that everybody in his kingdom had to fall down and worship this principality. Daniel, Shadrach, Meshach, and Abednego refused to bow down and worship this Babylonian god. No matter how powerful he may be he was not anywhere near their God.

This god was nothing in comparison to the God of the nation of Israel. These young men stood faithful and eventually Nebuchadnezzar gave a testimony to the God of Daniel. He said truly if there is a god in heaven it is the God of Daniel. There is no god but Daniel's God.

What happened? Daniel prayed against that strongman over Babylon and it was bound. Jehovah came forth as the only true God, and the God of the Israelites became the God of Nebuchadnezzar. Then the Medes and the Persians conquered Babylon. The angel over the nations of the Persians and the Medes wrestled against Gabriel and held Gabriel for twenty-one days. It just proves strongman over these nations had power. He had strength until one greater than him came, which was Michael the great archangel of the Lord who was over the nation of Israel, the defender of the nation of Israel.

Michael came down and warred against this prince while Gabriel was able to slip down and give the message to Daniel. God reviewed this in the Old Testament for us to understand that the powers that be are in the atmosphere above the earth. Earthbound spirits take their orders or their instructions from these spirits in the atmosphere.

Therefore, when we are praying for somebody and trying to do deliverance, we should always spend time in prayer before we begin the deliverance. I am not saying to just pray for a few hours or even a couple of minutes. If we have to, spend days in prayer asking the Lord to go before us and bind the strongman as we bind the earthbound spirits. The victory will be given to us, especially if you know the name.

Asmodeus, is the spirit of lust,
rebellion and perversion

Chapter 7
The Names are Important
>>>>>>>>>>>>>>>>>>>>>>>

There is a spirit called *Amazarak* who taught the art of sorcery and the dividing of roots, which means the mixing of herbs. He is a strongman that introduced the occult science into civilization. He also introduced the mixing of herbs to produce drugs. So he is the spirit over *pharmakeia* in the Greek or drug abuse in English. He is the spirit over witchcraft, sorcery, and spell casting. Therefore, when we are praying for someone to be set free from the spirit of witchcraft and we know the name of the spirit that introduced it into the civilizations of the world, then we can call that spirit by name and we'll get his attention.

This strongman is going to do one of two things when we call him by his name. He's either going to run or he's going to stand and fight. However, he will be bound in the name of Jesus and he will be cast aside. The person seeking deliverance that we are praying for will be set free.

When we're dealing with a spirit of murder there is a strongman that taught men how to make swords, knives, shields, and breastplates. He taught them how to make these things so men would fight among themselves and kill each other. Therefore when we know this particular spirit's name and we call him by that name, we get his attention.

We may ask, Brother Lewis, why is it necessary to know the name of these strongmen or these watchers?

When we pray, we must be focused and single-minded.

We must know that we have an enemy we are in combat with.

Next we should know his name so when we call his name we can get his attention and bind him in the name of Jesus.

We will get the victory instead of just second-guessing what is going on.

In today's society there are all kinds of books written about the Jezebel spirit, the spirit of lust, and the spirit of perversion.

People are coming against this spirit and calling it by a woman's name, Jezebel. What was the spirit which influenced the woman, Jezebel, to act the way she acted?

What spirit taught her how to dominate her husband, *Ahab*, take control of the kingdom, resist God, and worship Baal?

There had to be a spirit showing her how to do these things. Jezebel was only a human being. She was not a spirit, yet when a very dominating woman comes into the church we automatically label it a Jezebel spirit and we say that this is the strongman. It's a strongman but it's not the real leader.

Asmodeus

You have to go to *Asmodeus*, the spirit of lust, rebellion and perversion. When you bind that spirit then you take the power away from the *Jezebel* spirit that's getting its authority and its strength from the spirit that is above her. We are running around binding little private demon spirits while we let the generals go free.

42

I RESPECTFULLY DISAGREE

I know there are good books out there by pastors who teach that we should not mess with the strongman. They say we should deal with the earthbound spirits and leave the strongman alone because that's God's problem. I respectfully disagree because we have the authority to bind and to cast down anything that exalts itself against the Lord. We can do this as long as we are not picking the battle and saying we're going to take this spirit on. If we do that then we're going to lose every time.

Why? We'll lose every time because we'd be doing it in pride and arrogance. We are really trying to boast of our great spiritual strength when we say that we're going to do this or that and the Lord has not instructed us to do it. A word of warning – don't even bother with the earthbound spirits when you have an attitude like that because you will end up like the seven sons of *Sceva*. You will be running away naked and completely and totally beaten.

Strongman over Family Lineages

However, when the Lord says, "I want to use you to set this person free and I want you to pray for this person." Then, we must find out the name of the strongman that's over that person and their family. We don't need to be afraid of that battle because that battle is not ours. It's the Lord's and we are just the instrument or the vessel that the Lord has decided to use.

For some reason or another He trusts us enough that we will do this the way He wants us to do it. Not only will we bind the strongman but also we'll set the people free.

(Matthew 18:18) The Bible says that these signs will follow those that believe in My name.(Mark 16:17) They will cast out demons.(Mark 3:15) It does not just say, well, they'll cast out the little ones but the big ones they won't have any power over.

It says everything that exalts itself against the Lord we have the power and the authority to tear down, not in our own strength, but in the strength of the Holy Spirit and in the authority of the name of the Lord Jesus Christ and the power of the blood.

Jeremiah 1:10 Today I appoint you to stand up against nations and kingdoms. Some you must uproot and tear down, destroy and overthrow. Others you must build up and plant."

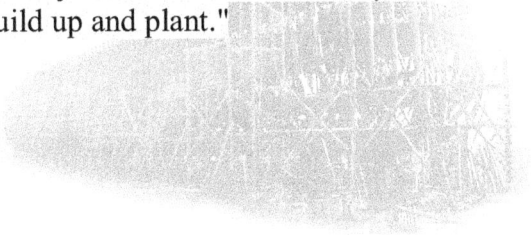

Chapter 8
The Ancient Spirits Are Returning
>>>>>>>>>>>>>>>>>>>>>>

They returning ancient spirits of old that are wicked and they are going to bring this earth back to the same condition it was under. Like the time of Noah, wickedness will abound everywhere.

When the Lord takes His church from the face of the earth, it will even be worse than what we are seeing today. Not only are the ancient spirits of old returning, but also the Ancient of Days, the Lord Himself, is returning. And there is no spiritual strongman strong enough to stand in the way of the Lord God.

The Lord is returning and He's returning the strength and authority to His church because the church is the body of the Lord on the face of the earth. He's giving the strength back to us to do the things He's commissioned us to do. So don't ever be afraid of any spirit because there is no spirit, no matter how strong it thinks it is, can

46

overcome our Lord. The strongest of the strongmen, Lucifer or Satan, is no match for the Lord God.

Lucifer was thrown out of heaven by another angel, and it was an angel of lesser authority than himself. Lucifer had the greatest position in heaven and the greatest authority given to any created being. Even Michael, when he was having a debate with Lucifer over the body of Moses in the book of Jude, said he did not dare bring a railing accusation against Lucifer. He simply said, "The Lord rebukes you, Lucifer. The Lord rebukes you; not I."

Michael knew where the authority was. It was not within Michael, even though he was a great and powerful warring angel and had already thrown Satan out of heaven. He knew the strength did not lie within him. It lied within God. The enemy may be able to debate against Michael and may be able to debate against you, or me but he cannot debate against God. He just can't win that battle, if we find out the name of the strongman.

People are running around trying to find out the name of this strongman and the name of that strongman. But who has the power over alcohol, narcotics, and cigarettes?

The One who has power over these things is the One whom we should be running to.

Why is it so hard to break these terrible habits of the flesh?

Amazarak

Well, *Amazarak* taught sorcery and the dividing of roots so anything that is addicting or any form of drug abuse, narcotics, alcoholism, and nicotine falls under his category.

Bind that spirit! Bind that strongman by name and watch what happens in the life of the person enslaved to it.

WE ARE NOT TO BE IGNORANT OF the
DEVICES OF SATAN: therefore NEED TO
UNDERSTAND the NATURE OF
RELIGIOUS SPIRITS.
IN GENERAL, RELIGIOUS SPIRITS ARE AT
WORK WHEN PEOPLE USE " RELIGION"
IN DEFENSE OF their WAYS AND SIN.

Religion and Traditional lies dismisses Biblical truth & God's Spirit which is used to usher in the anti-christ spirit

Here is the following

When someone says there is another way to God other than through Jesus, **Acts 16:17,** (The woman possessed with a spirit of divination literally declared that Paul was showing "a way" (Greek) to God which implied there were other ways. Many people believe that there are "many" ways to God such as:
in good deeds
living a good life
praying to a saint
belonging to a particular church
or becoming a martyr of their religion

John 16:6
Jesus answered, "I am the way and the truth and the life. No one comes to the Father except through me.

When one has a mystical belief about God, but has not submitted himself to Jesus as his Lord. **Acts 19:14** the spirits will not acknowledge you as they did Paul

Neither knowledge nor rituals make one a true Believer.

Colossian 2: 8-17
See to it that no one takes you captive through hollow and deceptive philosophy, which depends on human tradition and the elemental spiritual forces of this world rather than on Christ.

Mark 7:9-13 (Jesus said that the Pharisees made void the commandment of God through their traditions.)

Traditions often bring dullness to hearing the voice of the Holy Spirit, which eliminates the gifts of the Holy Spirit.

Denominationalism often takes precedence over the moving of the Holy Spirit.

When one tries to gain or maintain his salvation through doing good works rather than relying upon the grace of God found in Jesus. **Matthew 19:16-21**

False religions and even churches today often teach that one has to do such and such to be saved or to maintain their salvation. **Hebrews 6:1, 9:14** (Both scriptures declare that such are dead works).

Signs and Wonders are not the source of truth. Satan will use many people to deceive people. Exodus 32:24, Revelation 13:13-15

Baal was the same spirit that tried to take over Israel

Chapter 9
The Opposing Factor
>>>>>>>>>>>>>>>>>>>>>>

What is happening to the nation of America?

Why are we walking away from the truth of the Bible then seeking God? Why have we taken out the God who gave us the power to become a nation, who protected us war after war after war, who blessed us far beyond any nation on the earth, and who caused us to prosper so wonderfully? Why are we pushing Him out? There is a strongman over America who wants to enslave America. We need to seek the name of this spirit.

We need to find the name of this spirit of deception, this spirit of false religion, this spirit of the lie, and this spirit of anarchy. We will find it because we will know the spirit by its fruits. We might be able to hide our name for a season but we won't be able to hide our fruits and our true nature. By its fruit, we come to see this is the spirit called Baal. It is the spirit that wants to be worshipped as God. We may ask, Pastor Lewis, why do you say this is Baal?

Baal was the same spirit that tried to take over Israel

It tried to push Jehovah away from the nation of Israel and direct the attention of Israel to the worshipping of him. Israel and America are the only two nations which can be honestly say they were developing by the mercies and grace of the God of the Bible. Now this spirit, Baal, wants to be worshipped in the place of Jehovah and it's trying to push God, the God of the Bible, out of America and establish itself as God.

Baal never works alone

As we read in the Old Testament we start to hear names like *Chiun*, a god of destruction and murder over one of the nations that opposed Israel. There was *Dagon*, the god of the Philistines, who boasted he was greater than the God of the

Hebrews until one day the God of the Hebrews removed his head, hands, and feet. Of course we can't forget Moloch, the murderer of children.

All these strongmen are lesser strongmen over the authority of a spirit like Baal and they are working to bring this country into submission to this false spirit who proclaims to be god. Once we know this and we see what is happening, we can begin to bind this particular strongman in the name of Jesus Christ. We can break its power over America.

Let me tell you, my prayers alone cannot do it. The prayers of my wife and I together cannot do it. I wish it could because my wife and I would spend all the time we could in prayer against the spirits so that our country could be set free. It's going to take a unity of all believers of all denominations to say we are tired of this.

Recently our president said we are no longer a Christian nation, but we are a nation of many faiths. That is not true! He does not have the rights to turn this country over to Baal. This is a Christian country because that's where our roots are. There is no God in America but the God of the Bible. There are other gods trying to push their way into it.

Church, we must join together and put aside our spiritual prejudices and pride. We must stand together shoulder to shoulder as a mighty army, which the church is, with banners held high and begin to petition God. We need to begin to declare, "There is no god but our God. There is no lord but the Lord Jesus Christ. There is no place in America for any god but the God of the Bible. We will bow our knees to no god but to the God of the Bible and to the true God of America."

We can do this if we work together. Now we know the name of the strongman trying to drag this country down, and the names of the strongmen that are working with him.

For example, abortions, there are 45 million babies sacrificed every year to *Moloch* the god of sacrifice.

Murder and chaos sacrifice to *Chiun,* the god of violence.

False religions and their alters are being established everywhere and sacrifices are made to *Dagon and Baal*, the false gods of religion.

We know their names, we know who they are, and we know what they want to do. It's about time that we tell the returning ancient spirits there's no room in America for you.

There's no room in our families, in our churches, in our schools, and in our government for you in the name of Jesus Christ, the King of kings and Lord of lords, the true God of true gods.!

We bind you and we command you to go from and leave this country alone.

We ask you Lord to influence the political parties to be influenced by the power of your spirit and to change the hearts towards you..

You might think I'm a little crazy or a visionary but if you will join me in faith and then join other true believers in faith, we can set our country free for one last great revival.

Chapter 10
Important History
>>>>>>>>>>>>>>>>>>>>>

Anakim
>>>>>>>>>>>

Anak means long neck and he was a giant and the son of *Arba* the founder of *Kirjath-Arba*. He was also the founder of a race of giants called the *Anakim*. The *Anakim* were a terror to the children of Israel (Numbers 13:22, 28) but were driven out by *Caleb*, who came into possession of *Hebron* (Joshua 13:13, 14).

Nephilim- Giants
>>>>>>>>>>>

The *Nephilim* (Genesis 6:4, Numbers 13:33) were another race of giants considered to be demigods. They were the unnatural offspring of the *Bene Eloim* (sons of God) and the daughters of men. This utterly unnatural union violated God's created order of being. It was just a shocking abnormality as to necessitate the worldwide judgment of the flood.

Rephaim
>>>>>>>>>>>
Rephaim are spirits of the deceased giants.

It is a race first mentioned in Genesis 14:5. They dwelt in Asheroth Karnaim. More than likely it was probably not the same as *Ashtaroth*, the residence of Og. (Deuteronomy 2:11, 20; 3:11, 13; Joshua 12:4; 13:12; 17:15 along with the Perizzites Genesis 15:20)

Rephaim is also used for the dead. (Job 26:5; Psalm 89:10; Proverbs 2:18; 9:18; 21:16; Isaiah 14:9; 26:14, 19)

Names of giants we know from the Bible are: Goliath, Lahmi (Goliath's brother), and Og, giant king of Bashan.

Noah means rest and quiet. He was the son of Lamech and tenth in descent from Adam. He was a preacher of righteousness.

Giants and Other Strange Beings
>>>>>>>>>>

In Numbers 13:22, 28 we have the report of the ten of the twelve spies sent out by Moses to spy out the land. These men were very much afraid of what they saw. In fact they described everything they were afraid of.

They were afraid of the *Amalekites* dwelling in the land of the south. Then there were the Hittites, the Jebusites, and the Amorites dwelling in the mountains. Finally there were the Canaanites dwelling by the sea and the coast of Jordan. All these were tribes or nations of war, very fierce warriors and battle tested.

The Israelites were just the opposite of these violent nations. Yet with these nations covering the south, the mountains and the sea, there was an even greater enemy that struck fear deep into the hearts of the ten spies.

What was it? It was the giants called the Anakim, the offspring of the *Bene*

Elohim (sons of God) with the daughters of men. These giants were terrible and ferocious warriors. They were an unnatural creation and were not the creation of God.

These mutated creatures, formed by the relationship between the fallen enemies (angels) of God and the daughters of men were beings without spirits. They were very large and very strong.

Legends state that these ferocious creatures were cannibals with unsatisfying appetites. According to them meat was meat no matter if it was a bird, fish, sheep, rabbit or even man. When they were hungry anything was considered food.

The sad story was that the *Anakim* were not the only giants in the land. There were also the *Nephilim* (Genesis 6:4; Numbers 13:33). These giants were so large and strong they were considered to be demigods. I believe that from this particular race of giants is where the fables of the Roman, Greek, Egyptian, and Norwegian gods are based on.

For instance, *Nimrod,* believed to be
a *Nephilim,* was known as the mighty
hunter before God.

From him we get the legend of
Osiris and *Heracles.* From *Nimrod's*
mother, *Semiramis,* we get the foundation of
all goddesses like *Isis.*

She is also portrayed in the world
famous statues of the Madonna and the
Christ child, which is proclaimed by the
Roman Catholic Church to be Mary and the
infant Jesus. The title "Queen of Heaven"
supposedly refers to Mary, the mother of
Jesus. The Madonna image and the title,
queen of heaven is actually given to
Semiramis and her son *Nimrod* named
Tammuz.

Nimrod's uncle killed his nephew,
Nimrod, therefore; Nimrod's wife,
Semiramis, informed anyone who would try
to take her life that the constellation of
Orion was the spiritual body of *Nimrod.*

According to her, *Nimrod* was now
returned to heaven to watch over her and

their son, *Tammuz*, who was now the sun
god. She proclaimed all this in order to
protect herself.

It is quite amazing how the unholy
trinity of *Nimrod* was formed and introduced
to the world of men.

The unholy trinity was: Nimrod,
Semiramis, who was his mother and also his
wife, and their son, Tammuz.

Semiramis became the image of the
holy mother, Mary while *Tammuz* became
the image of the blessed infant, the very
incarnation of his father *Nimrod.*

After his death, *Nimrod* was
recognized as the constellation of *Orion*.

The story of the unholy family can
be found in the various legends in each
culture just like the story of the flood is
found in all the religions of the world.

Legendary heroes like Heracles,
Balder the Brave, Orion, Osiris, and Bacchus
can all be traced back to Nimrod.

Interestingly the fashion of wearing horns to show power and strength began with *Nimrod*. The images of him with horns and bull feet became the image of the Christian devils.

Every root from Nimrod, every false religion comes forth including a Nephilum.

I realize I have taken extra liberty with explaining more about Nimrod; however, we must understand that from the **root of Nimrod, a *Nephilim* comes every false religion that has been created**.

From the religions of Babylon, to Egypt, to Rome, to Greece, and to India he was the man who introduced the occult back into the world after the flood.

Who is the famous giant in the bible?

If I asked the average Christian who is the most famous giant in the Bible, many would answer Goliath or maybe Og, king of Bashan. They would be wrong because the answer is *Nimrod*.

To get an even greater understanding or an in-depth teaching on Nimrod and his family,
I highly recommend reading Alexander Hishops book, The Two Babylons.

Nimrod was responsible for the separation of mankind and the division of language among them. It was his pride and arrogance that made him think he could rise above God. Like his spiritual father, Satan, *Nimrod* was cast down and all his efforts were destroyed.

Nimrod, Lahmi (Goliath's brother), Og and Goliath were giants after the flood but what about before the flood?

Chapter II
Giants Before the Flood
>>>>>>>>>>

Although we do not know the name of individual giants before the flood, we do know who their fathers were. In the <u>book of Enoch</u>, which was uncanonized after the ninth century by the Roman Catholic Church, we are given the names of the twenty of the leaders of the *Bene Elohim* (sons of God).

There is also a list of the other two hundred fallen angels that follow them.

However I have listed only the names of the leaders or watchers

Names of the Watchers

1. Samjaza
2. Artaqifa
3. Armen (Rameel)
4. Kokabel
5. Tarael
6. Ramyal
7. Danjal
8. Neqael
9. Baraqel
10. Azazel
11. Armaros
12. Batarjal
13. Hananel
14. Ananel
15. Turel
16. Simipestel
17. Jetrel
18. Tamael
19. Arasel
20. Romael

There are many things that these fallen sons of God taught mankind. For example,

Azazel taught man how to make swords, knives, and shields. He taught them all about the metals and how to work them. He also taught the beautifying of the eyelids, precious stones and all kinds of colored dyes.

Semjaza taught enchantment and root cutting.

Armaros taught the resolving of enchantment.

Baraqyal taught astrology.

Kokabel taught the constellations.

Ezeqeel instructed man on the knowledge of the clouds.

Araqiel enlightened man to the signs of the earth.

Shamsiel educated man on the signs of the sun while

Sariel did the signs of the moon.

Kasdya taught women how to terminate lives in their wombs. In other words he showed them how to destroy the baby in the womb, which is what we know as abortion.

During the time of *Noah* there were three lineages of giants.

And when the food supplies became low they turned on each other destroying themselves.

The spirits of these giants became evil spirits that will roam the earth until the great Day of Judgment.

In the days of Noah the whole world was in chaos and rebellion. Men did that which they thought was right. They made images of gods out of stone, wood, or even precious metal.

These fallen sons of God also taught men fornication, lesbianism, homosexuality, and sex with animals. Perversion was widespread as was drug abuse and alcoholism.

Incest was ramped. Sex with children as well as with the dead were prevalent.

Disorder ruled unchallenged,
spiritual darkness was all over the earth, and
men welcomed the dark cloud of evil.
The only person not affected by all this was
Noah, a preacher of righteousness.

God ordered Noah to build the ark,
which gave man another hundred plus years
to hear the message of righteousness and
holiness. The Lord gave men a chance all
the way to the closing of the ark's door.

One minute after the door to the ark
was closed and sealed by God, the
foundation of the earth broke forth with
water and the heavens poured out rain on the
earth for the first time. The flood destroyed
all life, including giants and man.

According to Enoch the giants,
though they are physically dead, their spirits
are condemned to wander the earth as
unclean spirits or what we may call
earthbound spirits. From this we see the
origin of demon spirits.

The fathers of these giants are what we call principalities and wicked spirits in high places, powers, and the rulers of darkness. The sons, the giants, have become earthbound spirits which we call demons or spirits of sickness, blindness, or lameness.

This seems to be an answer to the spiritual opposition we face daily. Let me reiterate to help us in understanding the dark spiritual world. Satan is the prince and power of the air, the fallen angels are the strongmen, and the giants are the earthbound spirits. Without Jesus we do not stand a chance against this army of darkness.

Days of Sodom and Gomorrah
>>>>>>>>>>

So if all humans and the giants were destroyed in the flood, why are we in the mess we are in? The reason is Nimrod opened the door to darkness once again. The sons of God returned again to have relationships with the daughters of men and giants were back on the earth.

Wickedness once again covered the earth and men were once again doing what they felt was right in their own sight. Men built and continue to build images of false gods out of stone, wood and precious metal. Men continue to commit fornication and homosexuality and bestiality run rampant on the earth.

Homosexuals and lesbians controlled whole cities, like the cities of Sodom and Gomorrah.

They became so wicked that God had to destroy them. Can you imagine the foolishness of these men when they wanted so badly to rape the angels sent by God to Lot's house to deliver Lot and his family before God sent destruction to the cities

Instead of sending a flood to deal with the giant problem, this time God raised an army to face them and destroy them. The last giants killed were Og, Goliath, and his brother. Seems like God has handled all the problems, right? The earth should be blessed, right? No, man once again is in rebellion against God.

We have turned once more to false gods and goddesses. We have all kinds of occult science in the world. Witchcraft and homosexuality are twin spirits and they have the strongest lobbying parties in Washington D.C.

The return of the giants is upon us again

The world, as we know it, is turning back to the *days of Noah and of Sodom and Gomorrah*. The return of the giants is upon us again.

The rise of Nimrods grandson, known as the antichrist is at hand.

The Bible in the Old Testament refers to him as the Assyrian, which is no surprise since he is going from the city of his 3x great grandfather Nimrod. Every day we see the rise of evil in every kind of way from mass murder, rape, child abuse, and bestiality.

Men are celebrating all kinds of perversion and calling evil good and good evil. Men have become lovers of themselves than of God evil is running rampant throughout the land.

We have Jihad assassins who are trying to destroy America. We have mass killings occurring almost every day.

Loyal Police Officers are being gunned down who protect our neighborhoods and cities.

New Agers, occultists, and humanists are trying to push God out of America. Our president, Mr. Obama, has said we are no longer a Christian nation but a nation of many religions.

Religious leaders are compromising the gospel for the sake of numbers.

The prophets of Baal are spreading their religious lies everywhere.

Religion has replaced
relationship.

We know OF God, but we
do **not** KNOW Him.

Chiron is considered the most
supreme. It is Chiron who taught
Achilles in the art of war.

Chapter 12
Other Strange Creatures
>>>>>>>>>>>>>>>>>>>>>>>>

Within every society and religion there are legends or stories about creatures that are not fully human or fully animal. These legendary beasts are especially prevalent in Roman and Greek mythology.

The most famous are the centaurs, which are half man and half horse. According to legend they were mighty warriors and expert archers, and they ruled the forest where they lived.

Of all the centaurs, *Chiron* is considered the most supreme. It is *Chiron* who taught *Achilles* in the art of war. *Heracles* killed another famous centaur, *Nessus*.

Then we have the creatures we would refer to as monsters. One such creature is the *Minotaur*, which is the offspring of a human mother and a bull. His appearance was quite formidable especially since he had the head of a bull and the body of a man. He lived at the center of a special place called the *Labyrinth*.

King Minos of Crete demanded from King Aegeus of Athens seven female virginal girls and seven boys to be fed to the Minotaur. This happened for twenty-seven years until Theseus, the son of King Aegeus killed Minotaur.

It is amazing how the legends of these creatures of Rome, Greece and Norway have similar records in different cultures of the world's nations. For example we have the fable of the famous minotaur: a creature of the head of a bull and a body of a man. This very same type of creature is found in the records of Egypt god and war of destructor called Mont and his companion a creature with the body of a man and a head of a lion. This creature is also a **god of war** and massacre called *Maahes*.

My wife and a very strong prophetess from Africa both had a vision of these 2 creatures getting ready to run through Egypt to massacre Christians. My wife saw *Maahes* and the sister in South Africa saw *Mont*. Both spirits were coming out of the pyramid and running through the country.

We received the call for help from Christian brothers in Cairo that the Muslim brotherhood gave them three days to surrender their properties and convert to Islam or be killed. We called on everyone we knew to pray against these spirits. In three days times we received the news of a miracle. After binding these spirits by their name and in the name of Jesus, the Egyptian army overthrew the government and the Christians were protected. The army also promised to rebuild 700 churches that were destroyed under the former government.

Creatures like *Mont, Maahesh and Minotaur* may not be no longer seen in the flesh but they do exist in the spirit world.

Knowing the names of your enemy gives you power over them.

Another famous monster was *Medusa*. She was one of the three Gorgon sisters whose gaze turned creatures into stone. However, unlike her sisters, Euryale and Stheno, Medusa was mortal.

Medusa had penetrating eyes that mesmerized those who looked upon her and the unfortunate being was turned into stone. Instead of hair she had a head full of venomous snakes.

She had a large serpent tongue and teeth as long as the tusk of a boar. Her body was covered with scales that were so close together no weapons could pierce them. She also had golden wings and claws of brass.

Though she was terrifying and seemingly indestructible, *Perseus* finally tricked *Medusa* into looking at her image in his shield. When she looked in *Perseus'* shield she turned herself into stone and then was beheaded by him.

Pan was a creature who had the body of a young man with horns on his head and his lower half was that of a goat. He was a companion of Hercules and a god of shepherds, forests, wildlife, and fertility.

Pan was the son of *Hermes* and a fair-haired daughter of *Dryops,* one of the sons of *Apollo*. Along with these demigods there were also many other creatures not quite gods or immortals, yet neither fully human.

They were the *satyrs, nymphs, and the Silens*. The *Silens* were similar to the satyrs but were older and experts in music and prophecy. They were considered the gods of the forest.

The nymphs were divided into several categories. There were the dryad nymphs who lived in trees, hamadryad nymphs who inhabited oak trees, and *Meliai nymphs* who lived in ash trees

Water nymphs that lived in springs, brooks, rivers, fountains, or lakes were called *naiad nymphs*. There were also the three thousand daughters of *Oceanus* and *Tethys* who were sea nymphs or the *Oceanids*. Finally, there were the *Oreads* who lived in mountains and grottoes.

The Titans were giants with incredible strength that fought against the gods and goddesses. Did these strange creatures all exist at one time or another throughout history or are they just fables and man's imagination?

The Titans were actually the *Bene Elohim*, better known as the fallen angels. Their leader was a cherubim known as *Heylel*, who would become known as the adversary or better known as Lucifer among the Greek and Satan in the Gentile world.

This fallen angel, along with the angels he led in rebellion, tried to overthrow God and take over heaven. His plan failed drastically and Michael, the great defender of Israel, and the loyal angels that did not side with the adversary threw Lucifer and his angels out of heaven.

The giants in Greek and Roman mythology were actually the sons of the fallen angels and the daughters of men. These mutated beings made war on mankind and nearly destroyed all of mankind before the flood. However, God had his man who remained faithful to the Lord and his name was Noah.

For over a hundred years, God had Noah and his sons build an ark. During the time it took Noah to build the ark he preached righteousness and warned the people of the judgment to come. Men, giants, and other creatures ignored the warning and continued to do their own thing.

Still More Creatures to Come
>>>>>>>>>>

In the book of Job we have an account of some unusual creatures. They are *Behemoth, Leviathan* the great sea monster, and *Rahab*. These are all sea creatures who lived in the time of Job, which is believed to be the oldest book of the Bible.

These creatures lived in the rivers and sea and were feared by everyone. They were all invincible to the weapons of man at this period of time.

Modern man believes these creatures are the hippo and the crocodile. However, they were more than likely the brontosaurus, and in *Leviathan's* case, some kind of pre-Adamic sea monster.

Interestingly we find at the beginning of Job that there are two times when the *Bene Elohim* came together to give an account of what they were doing. Satan also came to bring accusation against Job.

When Satan was asked what he was doing he stated that he was walking to and fro over the earth. Therefore we know from scripture that Satan, at the time of Job, still had access to both heaven and earth. We also know that wherever we find Satan, we find trouble.

It is believed by some that before Adam there was another earth in which Satan, before his fall from grace, was the overseer of. If this is true then it is most likely that he not only turned one-third of the angels against God but also the population of the first earth.

God destroyed that earth with what is called the Luciferian flood. This particular flood is where everything was destroyed except for Lucifer and his fallen comrades.

Lucifer never gives up because when God recreated the earth and made Adam the judge and ruler over the earth, Lucifer once again struck out to destroy the earth.

In the Old Testament God told his people not to cross breed their cattle. God stated that each creation should bear seed after their own kind. God was concerned even about the animals being crossbred.

In many cases when animals are crossbred, they obtain both the strengths and the weaknesses of both species. The mule for instance is stronger than its parents, yet it is sterile and cannot reproduce.

If we look at the cross breeding of many of our dogs, we see that many breeds are sickly. They may look good but the overall health of these animals is poor.

Before the flood Lucifer went against God's plans for creation. He not only pollutes the human race but he also pollutes the animal kingdom as well as the water creatures.

In Greek and Roman mythology we have a creatures known as Sirens. These were winged women who used their songs to lure sailors to their death.

Along with the *Sirens* there are also legends dealing with mermaids and mermen. These creatures have the body of a handsome man or an attractive woman but the body of a fish. They lived in the oceans and the waterways of the world.

According to legend they could produce legs and come ashore for short periods of time and have relations with people thereby being able to keep their species going. The babies would be born normal but at a young age had be given to the sea were their mermaid parent would take them to their underwater world.

The Bottom of the Sea
>>>>>>>>>>

Atlantis was a place where civilization was so scientifically advanced. However, this place sinks to the bottom of the sea.

The people from Atlantis supposedly turned into *merbeings*, adding to the legend of the *merpeople* that was in the Harry Potter movie.

Among the Egyptians today some will not eat fish. They do this to honor *Derketo*, a Syrian goddess. Unlike the description of mermaids in other legends, *Derketo* is anatomically different.

These creatures are blamed for storms at sea, for heavy rains, and for great destruction on land and sea.

They are believed to have great cities on the bottom of the sea.

Their one weakness is that they fall in love with normal humans.

All of these mythological creatures existed before the flood and were destroyed by the flood of Noah. Therefore, if we observe the world before the flood, what we see is a world of absolute chaos.

There are creatures in the sea from so-called *merpeople,* the mighty Leviathan, *Behemoth, and Rahab, the giant squid.*

On land we have offspring of the fallen angels and the daughters of men called giants. These giants are killing and eating everything they can. Besides these giants we have legendary monsters that are part human and part animal, like the centaurs, pan-like creatures, and other mythological mutations.

God's word says that there was only one man and his family on the earth that was not touched by what was going on around him.

He refused to compromise with the world but rather stood strong with the Lord and willingly obeyed him.

I wonder what was going through the mind of Noah as he labored to build the ark and to preach to his generation. I wonder how this preacher of righteousness must have felt, after preaching for over a hundred years, he did not have one person respond to his message.

I know that before the flood there was no proof of the existence of these mythological creatures and the gods and goddesses or their offspring.

However, the giants did exist and it is from them we get the foundation of all false gods and goddesses.

The days before the flood was a time so evil that it sent a terrible odor in the nostrils of God day and night. It was a time so evil it caused God to repent for having made man.

It was a deplorable time filled with mass murders, thievery, adultery, and devil worship. There were pedophiles, transvestites, homosexuals, drug addicts, and alcoholics everywhere. Mankind was seeking after his own pleasure.

No one except one had a heart for God. Can you imagine it? Ninety-nine percent of the world population at that time had turned their backs on God and His ways.

Even though the flood destroyed all of the corruption on the earth, wickedness found a way to creep back in. For instance, there is an interesting legend about a giant named *Nimrod.*

It was said he killed a leopard with his bare hands. After he killed the leopard, he wore the skin around his shoulders as a sign of his great strength. Because the skin was spotted, *Nimrod* became known as the spotted one.

It was believed that the father of Nimrod was Bel. This name could simply refer to *Cush, a grandson of Noah,* who men refer to as a god and a prophet of the gods. However, many believe that the fallen angel, Bel, was actually the father of Nimrod.

Since *Bel* was a fallen angel, this is in all accounts would make *Nimrod a Nephilim*. It would also explain his great strength. These two facts would make Nimrod and the Greek and Roman demigod, *Heracles*, one and the same person.

Hercules and Heracles

Interestingly enough there is one small legend about *Hercules and Heracles*. The story says that Hercules killed a lion with his bare hands and from that moment to the rest of his life he wore the skin across his shoulders.

The funny thing about the skin of the lion is that it was spotted just like the skin of the leopard Nimrod killed. Just like Nimrod, Hercules' nickname given to him was the spotted one.

Upon the person of Cush, the father of Nimrod was the title, Bel the confounder. Nimrod became Orion and Semiramis, the wife and mother of Nimrod became the goddess of fortresses and she was also given the title, Queen of Heaven.

In Egyptian legend she was the dove, which is the symbol of the Holy Spirit. In the form of a dove she dove into the waters, and then she, as the Holy Spirit, purified the water for baptism. Both the Egyptian and the Babylonian worship the Chaldean queen of heaven.

In early Egyptian theology and early Catholic teaching the trinity consists of the father, son, and the mother. It was believed the father created everything then and was withdrawn away from his creation. The son was angry so you had to go to the mother for protection and answers.

Does this sound familiar? This doctrine was done away with until about the third century B.C. when the Roman Catholic Church revived it.

All of the false teaching that came from Egypt and Babylon was done away with when God chose a people to share truth with. Not only were the giants that were born after the flood destroyed by the newborn nation of Israel, but also the false teaching of Egypt and Babylon.

God now had a special people separated from the rest and from whom He could bring forth the promised Messiah. These people were to stay separate from all other people and they were to obey the laws and commandments of God.

The enemy tried and tried again to destroy them. When that failed he tried to get them to intermarry with other people. By doing this he would cause them to be polluted and to lose their relationship with God.

Time after time God had to discipline His people so He could bring them back to Him. Just as through one man the world was saved and repopulated after the flood, it was through one man, Abraham, that God was able to rise up a nation to establish righteousness.

The enemy knew that if he could not destroy or alter this nation of separate people they would be able to influence the

94

rest of the world. They had already destroyed the giants. And the sins of homosexuality and witchcraft were not allowed in their nation. If this nation was not done away with, the promised Messiah would come through them and salvation would be available to all men.

Though he tried, Satan could not stop the coming of the Messiah. The people who came to Him were all forgiven and an army of holiness began spreading throughout all people.

The battle seemed to be all over to the enemy but he and his legion of fallen angels came up with a diabolical idea. He would form his own religion that would closely resemble the religion of God. It would have its own priest and even use the Bible of God to enslave the people who were ensnared in its ways.

The major difference between the adversary's religion and the true faith was his religion's roots were in the ways of Babylon and Egypt. The true faith's roots went to the ways of Christ the Jewish

Messiah. His Jewish disciples were solidly rooted in Judaism.

The enemy promoted this so-called Christian religion but it is really a combination of many false religions along with Christianity. Satan also took polluted special days from various religions and made them into holidays that we celebrate, yet they are loaded down with his paganism.

For instance, Christmas is supposedly the birth of Christ. Wrong! It was actually the birth of Tammuz, the son of Nimrod and Semiramis who became the sun god.

Satan introduced a new character, which was all knowing, and would reward or punish according to how you behaved throughout the year. To do this he used the life of a god-fearing man named *Nicholas,* who once a year went throughout his village and left small gifts in honor of Jesus.

Satan perverted his sincere efforts to honor Jesus and turned him and his memory into Santa Clause, the big idol. He was even given to God's people, Jew or Gentile, and they replaced the pagan holiday with Christian terms.

In these last days you will see the Roman Catholic Church reach out to all the religions of the world and embrace them as members of the Church of Rome. Already the Anglican Church of England has asked to return to the Church of Rome and so has the Episcopal Church. The Lutheran Church has sued for the rights to return and even the Methodist Church has shown signs of wanting to go back to Rome.

The Pope of Rome and the leading Imam of Islam have met and are working out a way for the two religions to become one. It will not be difficult since both deny the divinity of Christ and both put a man in the place of Christ.

The Muslim say that Mohammed was the greatest of all prophets, even Christ, and Christ cannot be the Son of God because Allah has no son. The Roman Church has put the pope in the place of Christ stating that the pope's word bears more authority than the word of Christ or even the Bible.

When these two giant religions join together you will have the political leader known as the antichrist and the spiritual leader known as the false prophet rise up.

Then once again the world will be in great darkness and the creature that existed before the flood will return for the last seven years. The ways of Sodom and Gomorrah will cover the earth. Homosexuality and witchcraft will spread everywhere, and mass murder, robbery, and drug abuse will affect everyone on the earth.

One simple question I would like to ask is: are you ready for the coming of the Lord from heaven? I promise you that you will not want your sons or daughters as well as yourself to be here during these last seven years.

Yes, the ancient spirits that existed before the flood and in the days of Sodom and Gomorrah are all coming back

BUT SO IS the ANCIENT OF DAYS, which is our Lord and Savior Jesus Christ.

Keep looking up for your redemption is drawing close!

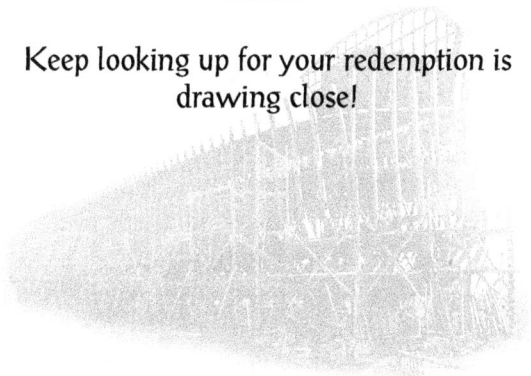

Chapter 13
Pre-Adamic Creation
>>>>>>>>>>>>>>>>>>>>>

Rebellion and overthrow of the first social
system
(Genesis 1:2; Isaiah 14:12-14; Jeremiah
4:23-26; Ezekiel 28:11-17; 2 Peter 3:5-6)

Earth's first sinless career
(Genesis 1:1; Ezekiel 28:15)

The anti-chaotic age extends from
the original creation of the heavens and the
earth; and everything within to the rebellion
and overthrow of the first cosmos, the first
social order on earth. It was the dateless
period from Genesis 1:1 when the earth was
finished and inhabited in the beginning and
Genesis 1:2 when the earth was first flooded
destroying all lives therein.

It involves that unknown time during
which the earth was in its first state and was
under the leadership of Lucifer before he fell
and caused the earth to be completely
flooded and destroyed. There is a difference

between the flood of Lucifer when he ruled the earth and led the rebellion against God and the flood of Noah when Lucifer causes the second flood to happen when he corrupts Noah's world.

The flood of Lucifer's was more destructive than even the flood of Noah because in the first flood even the vegetation was destroyed whereas Noah's did not (Genesis 2:5-6; Jeremiah 4:23-26). There are twenty differences between the flood of Lucifer and Noah's flood.

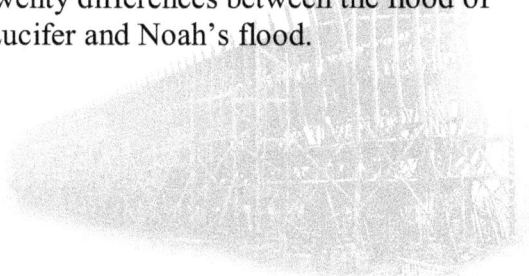

The Flood of Lucifer
>>>>>>>>>>

1. Lucifer's earth was made waste.
(Genesis 1:2; Jeremiah 4:23)
2. Earth was made empty.
(Genesis 1:2; Jeremiah 4:23)
3. Earth was made totally dark.
4. There was no light from heaven.
5. There were no days
(Genesis 1:2)
6. All vegetation was destroyed.
(Jeremiah 4:23)
7. There was no continual allotting of water
off the earth.
(Genesis 1:1-16)
8. Water is taken off in one day.
(Genesis 1:10)
9. There is a supernatural work of removing
water off.
(Genesis 1:6-12)
10. God rebukes the water.
(Genesis 1:6-12; Psalm 104:7)
11. Water hastens away.
(Psalm 104:7)
12. God sets bounds for waters.
(Psalm 104:9)

13. All fish died because sun was withheld from the earth.
(Genesis 1-2; 20-23; Jeremiah 4:20-23)
14. No fowl is left.
(Genesis 1-2; Jeremiah 4:23-26)
15. No animals are left.
(Genesis 1:24-25; 2:19)
16. No men are left.
(Genesis 1:26-28; Jeremiah 4:23-26)
17. No social system is left.
(2 Peter 3-6; Jeremiah 4:23-26)
18. No ark is made to save lives.
(Jeremiah 4:23-26; 2 Peter 3:6-7)
19. The cause of the flood was the fall of Satan.
(Isaiah 14:12-14; Jeremiah 4:23-26;
Ezekiel 28:11-17; Luke 10:18)
20. The result of the flood was that God had to recreate all things.

Many believe that the Pre-Adamic race is the demon spirits of today.

Noahs Flood
>>>>>>>>>>>

1. Noah's flood did not make waste.
   (Genesis 8:11-12, 22)
2. There earth was not made empty.
   (Genesis 6:17-22; 8:16)
3. It was not made totally dark.
   (Genesis 8:6-22)
4. There was light from heaven.
   (Genesis 8:6-22)
5. There were days.
   (Genesis 8:6-22)
6. Vegetation was not destroyed.
   (Genesis 8:11-17, 22)
7. Water receded naturally off of the
   earth.
   (Genesis 8:1-4)
8. Water took a month to be taken off.
   (Genesis 8:1-4)
9. It was a natural work of removing
   water from the earth.
   (Genesis 8:1-14)
10. There was no rebuke of the water.
    (Genesis 8:1-14)
11. Water recedes gradually.
    (Genesis 8:1-14)
12. The boundaries already set.

(Genesis 1:6-12; 8:2)

13. There were no fish were destroyed.
Only the land animals were
destroyed and the sun was not
withheld.
(Genesis 6:18-8:22)

14. The fowl were saved.
(Genesis 6:20; 8:17)

15. The animals were saved.
(Genesis 6:20-8:17)

16. Four men and four women were
saved.
(Genesis 6:8)

17. The social system was left.
(Genesis 6:18; 8:22; 2 Peter 2:5)

18. An ark was made to save lives.
(Genesis 6:14-22; 1 Peter 3:20)

19. It was caused by men's wickedness
(Genesis 6:5-13) and the sins of the
fallen angels (Genesis 6:1-14)

20. Result: no new creation had to be
made for all that was had a portion
saved   (Genesis 6:18-22)

To sum it all up, Noah's flood lasted over a year and yet vegetation was NOT destroyed.

However in the flood of Lucifer, the fruitful place became a dry barren place. (Jeremiah 4:23-26) Everything had to be done anew with the six days of creation because everything was completely destroyed. (Genesis 1:11-12; 2:5; 8:17)

This gives proof that the flood of Lucifer was on the earth longer than the flood of Noah and shows without a doubt a more serious judgment on the Pre-Adamic earth for a more serious crime than the time of Noah.

The whole Pre-Adamic race was judged and condemned to total destruction. The fact that Lucifer had previously ruled the Pre-Adamic world added to his jealousy of Adam. After all, Adam was a creature made from clay and he would replace Lucifer as ruler of the new earth.

There would be no way for this to happen if Lucifer had anything to say about it. He was already condemned once and everything taken from him. Therefore, in his clouded mind, he had nothing to lose and everything to gain.

Once again he is wrong!

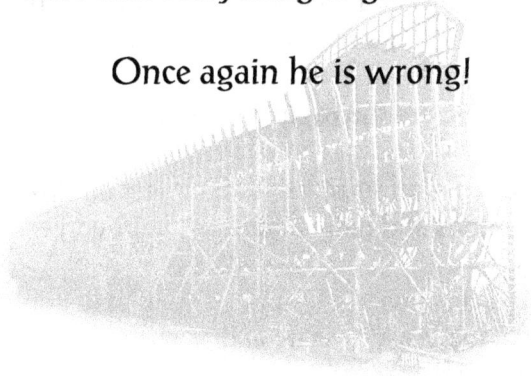

Chapter 14
America
God shed His grace on Thee
>>>>>>>>>>>>>>>>>>>>>

**Your enemies have weakened you.
The gates were opened inviting other
religions and their alters to come in. The
gates must be closed.**

You are the eagle on the ground!

**The remnant must rise to their feet out from
traditions and religion and battle in prayer**

Psalms 91:3 Surely he will save you
from the fowler's snare and from the deadly
pestilence.

Compromise of the word, religion and
the spirit of this world is blinding you and
deafening your ears to the truth of the word
of God and the voice of his spirit. The spirit
of discernment is being removed. The ears
of the people are being deafened and the

eyes cannot see to what is happening of what satan's plan is unfolding.

They seek to destroy you. If they do this, there will be no one to stand by Israel at their time of trouble. Our political leaders have betrayed us.

It is time for our people who know the Lord and hear his voice to stand in the gap and intercede for our country. It is the time for *2 Chronicles 7:15* to happen.

Let us wake up for the final trumpet is about to sound and god's bowls of judgment is about to fall. when god closes the door to the ark this time i hope you are on board and not left behind.

The word revival is being sought after but there is a price to pay for this.

It's called to be willing to be crucified with Christ, (Galatians 2:20) have been crucified with Christ and I no longer live, but Christ lives in me. The life I now live in the body, I live by faith in the Son of God, who loved me and gave himself for me.

To be challenged in prayer daily.

...but the people who know their God will display strength and take action." Daniel 11:32

One of the greatest needs in the Christian community is for Christians to discover and experience the privilege and power of effective prayer.

The one whose walk is blameless, who does what is **righteous**, who speaks the truth from their heart; Psalms 15:2

Do not conform to the pattern of this world, but be transformed by the renewing of your mind. Then you will be able to test and approve what God's will is--his good, pleasing and perfect will. Romans 12:2

We must carry the marks of being a committed Christian as Christ did. *(for I bear on my body the marks of Jesus. Galatians 6:17)*

These trying days of weariness
that we face today, many ways are
presenting themselves to be of God but
without discernment, we can be led off
the path from Christ into a universal
spirit of false unity

Chapter 15
What is the Strategy Now?

A plan of action or policy designed to achieve
a major or overall aim.

>>>>>>>>>>>>>>>>>

Praying for Revival
What does the word Revival mean?

Returning to the light or consciousness or to
the first love (Rev 2:4)

**It is about restoring LIFE BACK to the
believer of Christ** to be the lively stones
(I Peter 2:5)

*The word "revive" means to bring
back to life, or to restore. This is what
revival is supposed to be about. It is meant
to bring back or restore our relationship
with the Lord.*

Historically, revival meant something quite
different than what it is often called today.
In recent times, revival seems to be focused
on emotional experiences, the love of God,

laughing, happiness, singing, and dancing. There is little attention given to the bold preaching of God's word. Some churches even schedule revivals. This is in great contrast to the revivals of the past.

Some of the greatest revivals in history, lead by such men as Jonathan Edwards, Charles Spurgeon, Charles Finney, etc...

They had one message: **repentance** and turning from the ways and lusts of the world

Please remember that Noah was the FIRST REVIVALIST and the people of his time was the first congregation to refuse to hear and obey the word of God

The word of God was boldly preached, and people became so convicted about the holiness of God and their total unworthiness, that they fell to their knees in sorrow, contrition, humility, and reverence for God. The floors of the meeting places would be filled with people laying on the floor weeping. People were not focused on God's love. They were focused on God's mercy.

115

And, what is it that breaks our fellowship and relationship with God? SIN. How do we bring back to life that fellowship and relationship? Confession and repentance.

GREAT REVIVALS OF The PAST **WERE NEVER "scheduled."** they happened suddenly and quite unexpectedly.

And when they occurred, whole cities and counties were miraculously transformed. As these Christians became renewed in their walk with the Lord, they often found great joy and a renewed passion to share the gospel with the lost. This resulted in many others coming to faith in Christ. It is important to understand this point. In revival, one cannot be revived that was never alive.

In other words, revival isn't about reviving or renewing non-Christians, since they have never been alive in the first place,

but rather, it is about restoring LIFE BACK to the Christian.

The salvation of non-Christians is not what revival is about; however, it may be a byproduct or result of it.

Living a spirit led life by knowing and acting on the voice of God and being obedient brings maturity and a refinement of the character we need in order to be LIKE HIM. If we are not discipled, we will follow the whims of doctrine and religion having a form of godliness but denying the power thereof. In saying that: how can we be his deliverers to family members and friends who are in bondage?

Some people believe that you can be a Christian and not have to be discipled. *Luke 6:4*

They become offended by those who stand against false teachings and whims of doctrines because they have been subjected to "seeker friendly" ideas that embrace everyone to be a Christian. These seeker friendly churches do not disciple.

The BOOK OF NEhEMIAh CONTAINS A GREAT EXAMPLE OF WhAT CAN CONSTITUTE A TRUE REVIVAL

When the believers in Christ turn back completely and wholeheartedly to the Lord in repentance, we will experience revival. So many Christians pray for this nation to experience revival and healing, but we must alter our ways and be willing to experience Christ and be conformed in every fashion.(Romans 8:29)

Be Born Again and not just saved.
(John 3: 3-7)

(2 Chr 7:14) says, "if my people, which are called by my name, shall humble themselves, and pray, and seek my face, and turn from their wicked ways; then I will hear from heaven, and forgive their sin, and heal their land."

THIS is the formula for revival and healing.

About the Author

Dr. Henry Lewis is the President of Joshua International, an apostolic ministry. Joshua International offers Biblical Leadership and Spiritual Overcomers teaching. Henry Lewis is Scottish and a Sicilian Jew. He is a descendent of Andrew Murray.

He is married to his wife, Patricia, for over 46 years. They have been in ministry since 1980 and have two children.

Dr. Lewis has authored 12 books. The first book was called Testimony of Victory later changed to Quest for Spiritual Power. Translated in Arabic and in French. The Arabic book was printed book and distributed to over 6500 Muslims in Cairo Egypt. The French book was translated in Switzerland and printed in France.

Dr. Lewis is a sought-after Apologetics teacher, speaker and author, teaching at churches and conferences along with numerous TV guest media outlets teaching on subjects such as: spiritual warfare, revival, revelation, transformational prayer. Henry teaches internationally.

His testimony of his former occult leadership experiences of seven generations has enabled him to share the love of God and his delivering power.

Charisma magazine shared is testimony in 2000. 750,000 Hindus translated the article in their language and accepted Christ.

Dr. Lewis attended several colleges which led to obtain three Doctorates in Counseling, Theology and Christian Education.

Henry and his wife have established churches in the US. Their first church was by the assistance of Aimee Semple McPherson's son, Rolf McPherson, who believed in their calling. Later, Dr. Roy Hicks, Sr. (friend who worked at Angelius Temple with Rolf McPhearson) supported them as well.

Henry and Patricia's spiritual foundation was formed from: Dr. Leonard Heroo (Apostle and President of Zion Bible Institute), McPherson), Evangelist Robert Schambach, Prophet David Wilkerson and Derek Prince, Lester Sumrall etc.

Henry's passionate thirst for the knowledge and truth of God's word led him to obtain a deep relational experience with his Lord and Savior, Jesus Christ – and not a religion – so he could hear and know the voice of God.

120

His vision is to teach and train a courageous generation the incorruptible Word of God and introduce the power of the Holy Spirit. Henry and Patricia's goal is to bring restoration to all nations including the Native Americans. His wife, Patricia is of the Iroquois nation.

Henry & Patricia coordinated large transformation events in New England under the 'Vision for New England" network which began in Salem, Ma with the help of Rev Ken Steigler & local pastors. Daystar programming promoted the events for 2 years. A transformation video was edited that shares the signs and wonders and miracles that occurred.

Dr. Henry Lewis is ordained with the Assemblies of God.
Henry is also ordained Rabbi through Asher Intrater from the Revive Israel Ministries

He is available for speaking.

For More Information

H.A.Lewis
Joshua International

P.O. Box 742
Kodak, Tenn 37764

Email: Info@halewis.org
Email: Info@ joshua-edu.org

To order or inquire of additional products, visit
us online

Website: www.halewis.org
Visit us on face book

Book Cover Artist: Debbie Wheat
Contact: izayu54@yahoo.com

Book Co-coordinators

Grace Miller
Patricia Lewis

Books

A Quest for Spiritual Power - Redeemed
from the Curse - testimonial
Choisi Par Le Maitre: En quête de puissance
spirituelle - (French translation)
A Quest for Spiritual Power -
(Arabic translation)
Nimrod - How religions began and how it
applies today
Spiritual Opposition to the Five Fold
Ministry
The Secret Names of the Strongmen - study
material & prayer manual- (300 Names)
The Dispensation of the Lion and the Lamb
The Return of the Days of Noah

Available on Amazon

Recommended Reading

Prayers that Move Mountains
by John Echardt

Revival Praying
by Leonard Ravenhill

The Two Babylon's
by Alexander Hyssop

One Nation under Attack
by Grant Jeffries

Praying Successfully
by Spurgeon CH

The Essentials of Prayer
by EM Bounds

www.ingramcontent.com/pod-product-compliance
Lightning Source LLC
Chambersburg PA
CBHW060528030426
42337CB00034B/1925